THE SERPENT'S TEETH

TWO PLAYS

DANIEL KEENE

Currency Press, Sydney

SydneyTheatreCompany

First published in 2008
by Currency Press Pty Ltd,
PO Box 2287, Strawberry Hills, NSW, 2012, Australia
enquiries@currency.com.au
www.currency.com.au
in association with
Sydney Theatre Company

COPYING FOR EDUCATIONAL PURPOSES

COPYING FOR OTHER PURPOSES

NATIONAL LIBRARY OF AUSTRALIA CIP DATA

Author:	Keene, Daniel, 1955–.
Title:	The serpent's teeth: two plays / Daniel Keene.
Publisher:	Strawberry Hills, N.S.W.: Currency Press, 2008.
ISBN:	9780868198385 (pbk.)
Other Authors/Contributors:	
	Keene, Daniel, 1955– Citizens.
	Keene, Daniel, 1955– Soldiers.
Dewey Number:	A822.3

Typeset by Dean Nottle for Currency Press
Printed by Ligare Book Printers, Riverwood, NSW
Front cover by Grant Sparkes-Carroll. Photo by Jez Smith
Front cover shows John Gaden and Joshua Denyer

Contents

The Serpent's Teeth was first produced by Sydney Theatre Company at the Drama Theatre, Sydney Opera House, on 19 April 2008, with the STC Actors Company

Directors, Pamela Rabe (*Citizens*) and Tim Maddock (*Soldiers*)
Set Design, Robert Cousins
Costume Design, Tess Schofield
Lighting Design, Nick Schlieper
Composer/Sound Design, Paul Charlier
Assistant Director, Cristabel Sved

Citizens:

RASID	John Gaden
TARIQ	Narek Armaganian, Joshua Denyer
BASIM	Peter Carroll
HAYAH	Hayley McElhinney
HABIB	Brandon Burke
SAFA	Amber McMahon
QASIM	Eden Falk
KAMIL	Ewen Leslie
YUSUF	Luke Mullins
INAS	Hayley McElhinney
SAMIRAH	Emily Russell
AZIZ	Steve Le Marquand
LAYLA	Marta Dusseldorp

Soldiers:

TOM LEWIS	John Gaden
JIM LEWIS	Luke Mullins
SAM LEWIS	Ewen Leslie
JACK LEWIS	Narek Armaganian, Joshua Denyer
BILL LEWIS	Peter Carroll
ROBERT HOLMAN	Brandon Burke
MARTIN HOLMAN	Eden Falk
EVE MELLICK	Marta Dusseldorp
HELEN SIMON	Amber McMahon
CATHERINE PAVIC	Pamela Rabe
JOHN BLACK	Steve Le Marquand
ALICE BLACK	Emily Russell
EMILY BLACK	Hayley McElhinney

But then Minerva came, that warrior's aid;
she glided from the sky and ordered him
to plow the ground and then to plant within the
the earth the viper's teeth: these were to be
the seeds of men to come. And he obeyed;
and even as he pressed his plow—as she
had bade him to—he scattered the snake's teeth
within the ground: from such seed, men would spring.
At that—a thing beyond belief—the ground
began to stir, and from the furrows sprang
spear-tips, then casques with waving plumes, and next,
shoulders and chests, and weapon bearing arms:
a harvest crop of warriors with shields...

And battle frenzy soon had seized them all;
at each other's hand, those brothers fell:
their wounds were mutual. Now those young men,
destined to such brief lives, beat with their chests
against their mother earth, warmed with their blood...

Ovid's *Metamorphosis*, Book III (Cadmus)
Translation by Allen Mandelbaum

CITIZENS

... truly what is my faith
except a stubborn voice
casting out its shining length to where I walk alone
sick and afraid and unable to accept defeat
singing as I was born to

from *Ode to Walt Whitman*
by Alison Croggon

CHARACTERS

RASID
TARIQ
HAYAH
BASIM
HABIB
SAFA
QASIM
KAMIL
YUSUF
INAS
SAMIRAH
AZIZ
LAYLA

ONE

Noon.

Pale earth and stone.

Rubble.

A high concrete wall.

A dusty path at the base of the wall.

Vast, clear sky.

Stillness.

Silence.

*An old man (*RASID*) enters.*

He pushes a wheelbarrow.

Standing in the wheelbarrow, its roots wrapped in damp hessian, a young olive tree.

*A young boy of about ten (*TARIQ*) walks beside* RASID.

RASID *stops and lowers the wheelbarrow about halfway across the stage.*

RASID: We'll stop. We have time. Is there any water left?

> TARIQ *takes a large plastic bottle of water from the wheelbarrow and hands it to* RASID, *who drinks.* TARIQ *watches him.*
>
> RASID *steps from between the shafts of the wheelbarrow and sits on a rock by the side of the path. He hands the bottle to* TARIQ.

You should drink as well. Just a little. We have a long way to go. There'll be plenty of water at the grove. And something to eat, I'm sure. They'll know how far we've come.

> TARIQ *only takes a sip from the bottle. He puts it back in the wheelbarrow.*

I'll rest a while. We don't have to rush. We have to get back by nightfall. But there's time for a little rest.

> TARIQ *stands between the shafts and tries to lift the wheelbarrow.*

No… it's too heavy for you… be careful…

TARIQ *struggles to keep the wheelbarrow balanced; it's on the point of tipping over.* RASID *quickly gets to his feet and rights the wheelbarrow.*

Put it down! It's too heavy for you!

TARIQ *drops the wheelbarrow and quickly steps away from it.*

The tree weighs twice as much as you… the earth around the roots is damp… that's what makes it so heavy.

TARIQ *stands staring at his feet.* RASID *approaches him and puts his arm around his shoulder.*

It's alright, Tariq, the tree isn't hurt.

TARIQ *doesn't move or respond.*

It's a fine tree, isn't it? I made sure to choose a very good one. Next year it will bear fruit. Maybe not much. But in a few years… well, if it's cared for properly… imagine the new olives hanging among the leaves.

TARIQ *glances briefly at the tree.*

Don't worry, Tariq, one day you'll be strong enough to lift a tree like this… when I'm too weak to lift one. But we have to get some meat on your bones! Look how skinny you are! You're like a blade of tall grass.

He pats TARIQ*'s cheek.*

Get me some more water. I've got such a thirst today…

TARIQ *fetches the water and gives it to* RASID, *who sits down again.* TARIQ *sits beside him.* RASID *drinks, then hands the bottle to* TARIQ.

Maybe we should have started out earlier. I didn't wake up until the sun was high. If we'd left while it was still dark we'd be almost there now. I sleep too much these days. I fall asleep in the middle of the afternoon. Why do I need so much sleep? I hardly work any more. Your father and mother do almost everything. I've been put out to pasture! Your mother was so against this whole… expedition. But Tariq will come with me, I told her. I'll have my best helper. Drink, Tariq, drink a little more. Your mother's a good woman, only she worries too much. But who can blame her? The way things are these days… what is there to do but worry? Put a little water on your face, Tariq, make a little cup with your hand. It's alright, we have enough.

TARIQ *splashes his face with a little water.*

One day we'll go to the sea. I'll teach you how to swim.

TARIQ *points at the wall.*

Yes, I know. The sea is on the other side. We'll have to find another sea… or go the long way around that… thing.

TARIQ *points off into the distance.*

Yes, I know. It's very long. But it must end somewhere.

TARIQ *hands the bottle back to* RASID, *who also splashes his face.*

That's good, that's very good. When I was your age my family lived not far from the sea. I'd swim almost every day. I'd run away from school to go swimming. I was no good at school, it made me miserable, but in the sea… I felt so happy. Once, Tariq, once there were no happier times. There was no need to look back, to remember. The happy time was the one you were living in. No time before had been better and the future… well, who thought about the future? Now everyone looks into their past to find their happiness and no-one dares to imagine the future… but once, it's true, there were no happier times.

RASID *takes a small drink from the bottle and hands it back to* TARIQ.

Let's get moving, before I talk any more. Sleep and talk, that's all I'm good for.

TARIQ *puts the bottle in the wheelbarrow.* RASID *stands between the shafts and lifts.*

I want to get home before dark. I want to see the look on people's faces when we get back and they see what we've brought. They'll be surprised, won't they?

>   TARIQ *smiles and nods.*

I want to see the looks on their faces.

>   RASID *pushes hard to get the wheelbarrow moving. He and* TARIQ *move off as the light fades to darkness.*

TWO

Early afternoon.

*As the lights rise again, a middle-aged woman (*HAYAH*) and an old man (*BASIM*) appear from the direction in which* RASID *and* TARIQ *have gone.*

HAYAH *walks behind* BASIM *holding aloft a large yellow umbrella, sheltering him from the sun. Both of them are dressed in black.*

HAYAH: Father… Father… Father…

BASIM: Yes?

HAYAH: Are you sure?

BASIM: I've told you that I am.

HAYAH: I'm only asking—

BASIM: Again.

HAYAH: I'm only asking again because—

BASIM: Because you don't listen.

HAYAH: I have listened.

BASIM: But you haven't understood.

HAYAH: That's my point.

>   *He stops abruptly and turns to her.*

BASIM: What haven't you understood?

HAYAH: Why—

BASIM: And why did you bring that ridiculous umbrella?

HAYAH: The sun's very fierce today.

BASIM: Why is it yellow?

HAYAH: It's the only one I could find. Well, I did find another one, a black one, but it was very small.

BASIM: A small, black umbrella would have done perfectly well. Not that I think we need an umbrella at all.

HAYAH: I just thought—

BASIM: I am not arriving at my brother's funeral under… that.

HAYAH: Well, until we get there… Father… why are we going?

BASIM: That's what you don't understand?

HAYAH: That's it.

BASIM: But I've told you. He's my brother.

HAYAH: You haven't seen him for twenty-seven years.

BASIM: So?

HAYAH: So… will anyone be expecting you?

BASIM: I was sent news of his death, wasn't I?

HAYAH: Yes.

BASIM: News of a death is always an invitation.

HAYAH: Is it?

BASIM: When I die will you come to my funeral?

HAYAH: But I see you every day.

BASIM: Will you be there at the graveside?

HAYAH: Of course I will.

BASIM: I find that very comforting.

He kisses her forehead.

HAYAH: You hate your brother.

BASIM: He was a hateful man.

HAYAH: Then why are you mourning him?

BASIM: Am I mourning him?

Pause.

HAYAH: I'm confused.

BASIM: News of a death is always an invitation. But not necessarily to mourn. I am going to my brother's funeral to say goodbye to him. We parted on bad terms and have lived in bad faith ever since. Neither he nor I would bend or forgive. If there was anything to forgive, or anything that could have been resolved by forgiveness. All that is now over. I now have only myself to forgive. And I haven't yet decided whether or not I will. I am going to my brother's funeral to stand by his graveside, to look at the faces of those who do mourn him, whoever they are, and to finally have done with him. I've waited for news of his death, now I no longer have to wait. My own death is all that need concern me now. It's very... liberating.

Pause.

You're a good daughter. But you're very stupid sometimes. Come. We'll be late.

He turns and moves off. HAYAH *follows.*

And get rid of that umbrella. I want to feel the sun on my face.

They are gone.

*After a pause a man in overalls (*HABIB*) appears from the direction in which* HAYAH *and* BASIM *have gone.*

HABIB *carries the yellow umbrella. He turns in the direction that* HAYAH *and* BASIM *have gone and waves to them. He calls out:*

HABIB: Thanks! Thanks again!

He looks up at the umbrella, admiring it.

What do you think of that? Fatimah will love it.

He holds the umbrella horizontally and twirls it; he walks quickly along the path, watching the umbrella spin like a huge, yellow wheel.

*A woman (*SAFA*) appears, carrying a large cardboard box.* HABIB *comes speeding towards her. She steps aside at the last moment, almost dropping the box.*

SAFA: Hey, watch where you're going, will you?

HABIB *stops.*

HABIB: Sorry!

He lifts the umbrella, shading both himself and SAFA.

Isn't it great?

SAFA: It's... very yellow.

HABIB: I'm going to give it to my sister. It's her birthday on Saturday. I had nothing to give her. Now I have this.

SAFA: Good for you.

The box is slipping from SAFA *'s arms; she struggles to keep hold of it.*

HABIB: Are you okay with that?

SAFA: It's heavy, that's all.

HABIB *closes the umbrella and lays it on the ground.*

HABIB: Let me help...

SAFA: It's okay, really...

HABIB: Here, just put it down for a minute...

He helps SAFA *put the box on the ground.*

It is heavy.

SAFA: It's an Alsatian.

HABIB: Pardon?

SAFA: It's an Alsatian. They're big dogs. Although she's not fully grown yet.

HABIB: A dog?

HABIB *looks down at the box.*

Is it dead?

SAFA: It's a she. She's asleep.

HABIB: Obviously she's a very sound sleeper.

SAFA: She's unconscious really. She's been given an injection.

HABIB: An injection?

SAFA: They didn't know how to treat her at the hospital, so they decided to sedate her. The doctor in charge was very kind. There's a veterinarian not far away. I have to get her there before she wakes up.

HABIB: What happened to her?

SAFA: She was hit by a car.

She stoops down to the box.

Can you help me?

HABIB: How far have you got to go?

SAFA: Jedda. Just over the—

HABIB: That's a long way.

SAFA: Then I'd better get going. Can you help me pick her up?

> HABIB *helps* SAFA *pick up the box.*

Once I've got hold of her properly… it's okay.

> SAFA *stands with the box in her arms.*

HABIB: How far have you come?

SAFA: Not very far. From Nazrin.

HABIB: Excuse me… but you don't seem to have much of an idea of distance. Nazrin is at least—

SAFA: Listen, I'm sorry, but I'm in a hurry. I don't care how far it is.

> *She sets off.* HABIB *follows her.*

HABIB: Don't you know anyone with a car?

SAFA: The man who almost killed my dog… he has a car.

HABIB: He should help!

SAFA: He isn't helping.

HABIB: Yes, but—

SAFA: But what? Will you leave me alone, please?

> HABIB *comes to a halt.* SAFA *continues on her way.*

> HABIB *pauses a moment. He runs back to the umbrella and picks it up. He hesitates a moment, then opens the umbrella and sets off after* SAFA.

> *The light fades to darkness.*

THREE

Mid afternoon.

*After a long pause, three young men (*QASIM, KAMIL *and* YUSUF*) appear from the same direction as* SAFA. *Each of the young men has a small sack slung over his shoulder. They stoop to gather stones from the side of the path, putting them in their sacks.*

QASIM: No, not that one, it's too big.

KAMIL: It's fine.

QASIM: It's too big.

KAMIL: The bigger the better.

QASIM: Don't be an idiot. How far could you sling it?

KAMIL: Far enough.

QASIM: Idiot.

KAMIL: Don't call me an idiot.

YUSUF: Would you two please shut up? You've been arguing ever since we left home.

KAMIL: No we haven't.

YUSUF: It really gets on my nerves.

QASIM: I can't help it if he's an idiot.

KAMIL: I'm not.

YUSUF: Did anyone bring anything to eat?

KAMIL: I've got a couple of oranges.

YUSUF: Only two?

KAMIL: That's all there was.

QASIM: We can share them.

KAMIL: Did you bring anything?

QASIM: No.

YUSUF: There wasn't anything to bring.

KAMIL: So we have to share my oranges?

QASIM: Is that a problem?

KAMIL: No.

YUSUF: So?

KAMIL: What if it was?

QASIM: But it isn't.

KAMIL: But how come you just… assumed I'd share my oranges with you two?

YUSUF: Why wouldn't you?

KAMIL: But I don't have to.

YUSUF: No. You don't have to.

QASIM: We're wasting time.

YUSUF: What's the rush?

QASIM: Can we just… get going.

YUSUF: We'll get there soon enough.

QASIM: It makes me nervous

KAMIL: What?

QASIM: Just… hanging around.

KAMIL: We need to collect our stones, don't we?

YUSUF: We don't have enough yet.

QASIM: We've got enough.

KAMIL: We need more.

QASIM: How many do you think we'll have the chance to use?

KAMIL: How do I know?

QASIM: Half a dozen, maybe. Then we have to run.

YUSUF: We know what we have to do.

QASIM: So let's do it.

KAMIL: If you're frightened then you should go home.

QASIM: I'm not frightened.

YUSUF: You sound frightened.

QASIM: Fuck you.

YUSUF: Fuck you as well.

KAMIL: Fuck both of you.

QASIM: This is great…

> KAMIL *takes a leather sling from his pocket, loads a stone from his sack and slings it at the wall. The stone shatters.*

> *After a pause:*

KAMIL: Let's go.

YUSUF: Can I have a piece of orange?

KAMIL: Sure… but just a piece.

> *He takes an orange from his sack and tosses it to* YUSUF.

QASIM: We should all have a piece.

> *They begin to move off.*

KAMIL: Okay. Just to be fair.

QASIM: That's right.

They are gone.

The lights fade to darkness.

FOUR

Late afternoon.

*Two middle-aged women (*INAS *and* SAMIRAH*) approach one another from opposite sides of the stage; they both wear hijabs. They both have large, black handbags slung over their shoulders.*

INAS *carries a small parcel under her arm.*

They stop a few metres from one another.

INAS: Samirah?

SAMIRAH: Yes. Inas?

INAS: Yes.

> *They approach one another;* INAS *holds out the parcel.*

Geography, history and mathematics.

> SAMIRAH *takes the parcel.*

SAMIRAH: I can't thank you enough.

INAS: My sister told me that you also needed a science book, but I don't have one.

SAMIRAH: This is already so generous. I've brought nothing for you. I wasn't really sure… I wasn't sure if you would come. So many arrangements… never amount to anything.

INAS: I understand.

SAMIRAH: But I must give you something in return.

INAS: I don't need anything.

SAMIRAH: Then you are a minority of one.

> *Pause.*

INAS: Do you have any salt? Or coffee?

SAMIRAH: No coffee. But salt, yes. Do you need flour?

INAS: I have a little.

SAMIRAH: Lemons?

INAS: Lemons?

SAMIRAH: My nephew brought me some yesterday, a whole bagful.

INAS: I'd like some lemons, just a few.

SAMIRAH: Half a dozen, and some salt.

INAS: And a little flour? Only if you can spare some.

SAMIRAH: Of course. Tomorrow?

INAS: Shall we meet here again?

SAMIRAH: There's no need. I'll send my brother. He has a motorbike. He has no fuel at the moment, but he has been promised some tomorrow morning.

INAS: It's expensive.

SAMIRAH: He teaches clarinet. One lesson for one litre of fuel. He's owed five litres. The boy he's teaching has no talent at all. His father is in despair, but his mother insists that he learns. My brother does what he can. The boy wants to be a lorry driver.

INAS: Where would he drive?

> SAMIRAH *shrugs.*

SAMIRAH: He's only a young boy.

> *Pause.*

These books are for my daughter. She wants to be a teacher.

INAS: Mine wants to be an archaeologist.

SAMIRAH: Thank you again.

INAS: Salwa has taken good care of them.

SAMIRAH: Zayna will take good care of them too. They'll go to her brother when she's finished with them. If there's still a school to go to…

INAS: Our school is closed right now.

SAMIRAH: Ours only has two teachers. They do what they can.

INAS: It's the same everywhere.

SAMIRAH: On this side of the wall.

INAS: Yes, on this side. But the other side is another world. I don't think about it.

SAMIRAH: Do you wonder if they think about us?

INAS: Now that they can't see us… we probably no longer exist. I don't care about them.

SAMIRAH: They were our neighbours not so long ago.

INAS: Do you have any water?

SAMIRAH: Yes, I have.

INAS: I'm sorry, I should have brought some...

> SAMIRAH *takes a plastic bottle of water from her handbag and hands it to* INAS.
>
> INAS *drinks;* SAMIRAH *watches her.*
>
> INAS *hands the bottle back to* SAMIRAH.

Thank you.

SAMIRAH: You're welcome.

INAS: My sister speaks very fondly of you.

SAMIRAH: I like her very much.

INAS: She told me... that you're alone.

SAMIRAH: Not completely.

INAS: But your husband...

SAMIRAH: Yes. I lost him.

INAS: I'm sorry.

SAMIRAH: So am I.

> *Pause.*

INAS: I should go.

SAMIRAH: My brother will come tomorrow.

INAS: It's the house by the old well. The one with the blue door.

SAMIRAH: He'll find it.

> *They embrace, briefly.*
>
> INAS *turns quickly and leaves the way she came;* SAMIRAH *watches her go, then turns, the schoolbooks pressed to her breast, and leaves the way she came.*
>
> *The stage is empty for a few moments.*
>
> *Somewhere far off, a dog barks.*
>
> *From the direction in which* INAS *left, a man and a woman in their twenties (*AZIZ *and* LAYLA*) slowly appear.* LAYLA *carries a suitcase and wears a small rucksack.* AZIZ *is pushing a shopping*

trolley; it's filled to overflowing with the couple's possessions: a large suitcase, a sewing machine, a rug, blankets, pots and pans, bundles of clothes, a portable television.

LAYLA *puts the suitcase down and takes off her rucksack.*

AZIZ: What are you doing?

LAYLA: We'll have something to eat and drink.

AZIZ: We have to keep going. At this rate, we won't get there until midnight…

LAYLA: Do you want me to push for a while?

AZIZ: It's too heavy for you.

LAYLA: I could try.

AZIZ: What's the point?

LAYLA: You need a rest.

> *She takes some bread out of the rucksack and offers it to him.*

Here… have something.

AZIZ: I don't want anything.

LAYLA: Suit yourself. I do.

> *She sits on the suitcase and takes a bite of the bread.*

> *After a pause:*

AZIZ: I'll have some water.

> *She takes a bottle of water from the rucksack, unscrews the cap and hands the bottle to him; he drinks.*

LAYLA: That's the last bottle.

AZIZ: We should have brought more.

LAYLA: You said that we had enough.

AZIZ: I didn't think that it would take us this long.

LAYLA: We're not even halfway there yet.

AZIZ: We're more than halfway.

LAYLA: I don't think so.

> *She shrugs.*

AZIZ: Less than halfway…

LAYLA: It doesn't matter what time we get there.

AZIZ: Have you forgotten about the curfew?

LAYLA: No. But the closer we get, the less the curfew matters. My cousin said the curfew isn't so seriously enforced around his village. Well, it hasn't been lately.

AZIZ: Things can change.

LAYLA: I know.

Pause.

AZIZ: Sometimes I wish that you'd worry a little more.

LAYLA: I don't have to. I leave that to you. Can I have some water?

AZIZ: Don't drink too much.

LAYLA: How much did you drink?

AZIZ: Just a few sips.

LAYLA: Then I'll drink the same.

She drinks; he watches her.

AZIZ: That's enough.

She takes the bottle from her lips, screws on the cap and puts the bottle back in the rucksack.

I'd like a little more.

LAYLA: You've had a drink.

AZIZ: I'd like another.

LAYLA: I told you, it's the last bottle.

AZIZ: Give it to me.

LAYLA: No.

He takes a step towards her; she remains impassive. He turns and walks away.

AZIZ: What else does your cousin say?

LAYLA: I've told you. He's found a house for us.

AZIZ: How many rooms?

LAYLA: Two.

AZIZ: No running water…

LAYLA: No.

AZIZ: No garden…

LAYLA: There's a small yard.

AZIZ: But no garden?

LAYLA: No, there's no garden.

AZIZ: I like to have a garden.

LAYLA: We'll have a garden again some day.

AZIZ: When?

LAYLA: I don't know.

Pause.

Aziz…

Pause.

AZIZ: What?

LAYLA: We'll have a garden.

Pause.

AZIZ: I'm sorry.

LAYLA: You don't have to be.

AZIZ: I don't want to move.

LAYLA: I know. I don't either.

AZIZ: Couldn't we have stayed… until the baby came?

LAYLA: It's better that we leave now. I want to have the baby where I feel safe.

AZIZ: Of course, of course…

LAYLA: Don't resent me for that.

AZIZ: I don't.

LAYLA: Are you sure?

AZIZ: Yes, I'm sure.

Pause.

I'm sure.

He turns and goes to her; she takes hold of his hand.

LAYLA: Good.

AZIZ: We should get going.

LAYLA: We mustn't resent anything.

AZIZ: No. We should get going.

They remain where they are; his hand in hers.

The lights fade to darkness.

FIVE

Early evening.

Empty stage.

Some distance off, YUSUF *is calling:*

YUSUF: [*offstage*] Qasim… Qasim… Qasim…!

> *Long pause.*
>
> YUSUF *runs on. His left shoulder is bleeding; blood runs down his sleeve.*
>
> *He calls again:*

Qasim!

> *He clutches his shoulder; he moves to the wall and slumps at its base.*
>
> *His mobile phone rings; it's in the left hand pocket of his trousers. He gets it out of his pocket with some difficulty.*

Hello? Hello? Kamil? No, I haven't seen him. Where are you? What are you doing there? What? No, I'm okay. I'm okay! Have you tried calling him? Me too. What? I can't hear you. Kamil? Kamil?

> *Pause.*
>
> *He stands up. He puts the phone in his right hand pocket.*
>
> *He looks left and right, uncertain of which way to go.*
>
> *He heads off the way he came, calling as he goes.*

Qasim… Qasim…!

> *The lights fade to darkness.*

SIX

Nightfall.

BASIM *and his daughter,* HAYAH, *are sitting on some stones at the side of the path.* HAYAH *is fanning her father with a white handkerchief. After a pause:*

BASIM: I wish you'd stop that.

HAYAH: But—

BASIM: It's very annoying.

>   *She stops fanning him; she wipes her face with the handkerchief.*

HAYAH: How do you feel?

BASIM: When did you last ask me?

HAYAH: I don't know…

BASIM: Whenever it was, I feel the same as I did then. I'm just a little tired.

HAYAH: Very tired.

BASIM: As you wish… I'm very tired.

>   *Pause.*

HAYAH: Everything… went well.

BASIM: There was almost no-one there.

HAYAH: How many people did you expect?

BASIM: More than there were.

HAYAH: Perhaps he didn't know many people…

BASIM: It seems not.

>   *Pause.*

HAYAH: At least you were there.

BASIM: There are so many deaths now. Perhaps people don't bother as much as they used to. A death used to be… something that people took some notice of. It's better to die in more peaceful times.

HAYAH: It's certainly better to live in them.

BASIM: How would you know?

HAYAH: There have been more peaceful times.

BASIM: But there has been no peace.

HAYAH: No, not really. But…

BASIM: But what?

HAYAH: One enjoys the moments one can.

>   BASIM *pats* HAYAH*'s cheek.*

BASIM: You are such a dear girl. But there have been too many tears. Every tear that falls is a serpent's tooth.

Pause.

I think that I can get up now.

She helps him to his feet.

HAYAH: Are you sure…?

BASIM: Yes, yes, I'm sure. I want to get home.

He takes a few, unsteady steps along the path, HAYAH *supporting him.*

HAYAH: Are you still glad that you went?

BASIM: It was my brother's funeral. How could I not go? It doesn't matter who he was. But I'm sad that he was so alone. I was sure that there would be people who would like him, even if I didn't.

HAYAH: I don't remember very much about him at all.

BASIM: He was tall. With very… bright eyes. He had… endurance. That was his gift.

HAYAH: You mean that he was as stubborn as you?

Pause.

BASIM: Yes, perhaps that's what I mean.

They slowly move off.

After a few moments, trailing behind HAYAH *and* BASIM, HABIB *and* SAFA *appear.* HABIB *carries the rolled umbrella over his shoulder.*

HABIB: We should catch up with them.

SAFA: No, I don't want to.

HABIB: But why not?

SAFA: They're in mourning.

HABIB: So?

SAFA: It's not our place to be with them.

HABIB: You seem to be… afraid of them.

SAFA: I suppose I am.

HABIB: But why?

SAFA: Because of something that my grandfather told me.

HABIB: What did he tell you?

SAFA: Do you really have to know?

HABIB: No. But I'd like to.

Pause.

SAFA: My grandfather told me that those who are in mourning… are caught between this life and the next… they're neither living nor dead.

HABIB: Of course they're not dead.

SAFA: Yes, of course.

HABIB: And of course they're alive.

SAFA: Do you want to hear what he told me or not?

HABIB: Yes I want to hear it.

Pause.

SAFA: They are neither living nor dead. They are both. It is as if they are standing in the doorway that separates those who are dead from those who are alive.

HABIB: What doorway?

SAFA: Will you please let me finish?

HABIB: Okay, okay.

SAFA: There is a doorway between the living and the dead… and all of us will pass through it. But when someone that we love dies… we are, for a short time… we are able to stand in that doorway, to see the death that awaits us and the life we will leave behind. It's love that makes this possible. Love… contains this doorway.

Pause.

HABIB: So why don't we catch up with them?

SAFA: For the same reason that you shouldn't wake up a sleepwalker.

HABIB: And what's that?

SAFA: Don't you know anything?

HABIB: I don't know anything about what you're talking about.

SAFA: You don't wake up a sleepwalker because the… the shock could kill them.

HABIB: But that's not true.

SAFA: So you know about sleepwalkers?

HABIB: I know what anyone knows.

SAFA: Well, you never knew my grandfather.

HABIB: No, I didn't.

SAFA: He said things better than I can.

> *Pause.*

You don't have to walk me home, you know.

HABIB: I know, but I said that I would.

SAFA: But you don't have to.

HABIB: I said that I would.

SAFA: It's up to you.

HABIB: That's right.

> *Pause.*

SAFA: Thank you for helping me today.

HABIB: It was no trouble. I hope that your dog will be okay.

SAFA: She will. She's strong.

HABIB: I can go back with you… to pick her up.

SAFA: If you like.

HABIB: Would you like me to?

SAFA: Why not?

HABIB: Sure, why not?

> *He opens the umbrella and holds it over their heads.*

Shall we go?

SAFA: Sheltered from the moonlight?

HABIB: Yes… sheltered from the moonlight.

> *They go.*
> *The lights fade to darkness.*

SEVEN

Night.

RASID *and* TARIQ *appear; they are going home.*

RASID *pushes the wheelbarrow.*

Standing in the wheelbarrow, its roots wrapped in damp hessian, a young orange tree. A small lamp hangs on one of the branches of the tree, casting a circle of light around the wheelbarrow (the shadows of leaves play against the concrete wall).

RASID: We'll soon be there Tariq. Soon…

    Pause.

Are you tired?

    Pause.

I'm tired. But it's been worth it. I was hoping to be home before nightfall. But it wasn't to be. I'm not so strong and swift as I was. I must sound so vain… but I was, I was strong and swift! That's what you'll be one day. Like an eagle!

    Coming to a halt, he lets go of the shafts of the wheelbarrow.

That's enough for now.

    He steps off the path and sits down on a rock. TARIQ *sits beside him.* RASID *puts his arm around* TARIQ*'s shoulder.*

You must be so tired, my dear. I'm sorry for that.

    He kisses TARIQ*'s head.*

I'm sorry for that. But you've been a great help. I couldn't have done it without you. A man needs company. Nothing is done alone.

    Pause.

Think of it… oranges in our village! There has never been such a thing! There's not much left of our olive groves… but we can plant this tree. They were very pleased with the olive tree that we brought them, weren't they? That pleased me. It was a fair trade. They're good people. The same family has been growing oranges for… for centuries. You like oranges, I know you do, when your mother can get them… well, in a while you'll be able to pluck them from your own tree. Think of that… Tariq?

    TARIQ *has fallen asleep against* RASID*'s shoulder.*

Sleeping…? My dear boy… but we have some way to go.

He strokes TARIQ*'s hair.*

It was foolish of me to bring you. Your mother will be so worried. I'll take the blame. It will be tiresome, but it will be just, I suppose.

He shakes TARIQ *gently.*

Wake up, Tariq… wake up…

TARIQ *stirs.*

You'll sleep soon, Tariq, but not yet.

TARIQ *nods.*

It's not far. Then you can rest.

RASID *stands and gets between the shafts of the wheelbarrow.*

Stay close to me. It's dark. This lamp doesn't give much light.

TARIQ *stands beside* RASID, *his hand on* RASID*'s arm.*

That's right. Stay close. We have a little way to go.

RASID *lifts the wheelbarrow and they set off.*

Shall I tell you a story? Just to pass the time?

TARIQ *nods.*

I'll see how much breath I have left. It may have to be a short story. Orange trees are heavy, and we have a little way to go.

They are gone.

Long pause.

From some distance off, the sound of a helicopter.

And somewhere far off, a dog begins to bark.

The sound of the helicopter slowly grows closer.

The bright circle of a searchlight hits the wall.

The sound of the helicopter grows even louder; it is hovering above the wall.

The sound of the helicopter drowns out the barking of the dog.

The spotlight moves back and forth along the wall.

The spotlight grows larger as the helicopter comes even closer; the sound is deafening.

Blackout.

Silence.

THE END

SOLDIERS

A REQUIEM

*Their souls became cold
and their wings fell slack.*

Sappho

*Why should a dog, a horse, a rat, have life,
And thou no breath at all? Thou'lt come no more.
Never, never, never, never, never!*

Shakespeare
King Lear, Act 5, Scene 3

CHARACTERS

TOM LEWIS, 60
JIM LEWIS, his son, 27
SAM LEWIS, his son, 25
JACK LEWIS, his grandson, 10
BILL LEWIS, his brother, 65

Tom is waiting for the return of the body of his eldest son, Steve, who was 32 when he died. Jack is Steve's son. Steve's wife, Sarah, has refused to be present at the return of her husband's body.

ROBERT HOLMAN, 45
MARTIN HOLMAN, his nephew, 23

Robert is waiting for the return of the body of his son, David, who was 21 when he died.

EVE MELLICK, 35
HELEN SIMON, 30

Eve is waiting for the body of her brother, Peter, who was 28 when he died; Helen was Peter's long-term partner.

CATHERINE PAVIC, 50

Catherine is waiting for the return of the body of her son, Rik, who was 23 when he died.

JOHN BLACK, 45
ALICE BLACK, 35, his sister
EMILY BLACK, his sister-in-law, 25

John is waiting for the return of the body of his brother, Alan (Emily's husband), who was 30 when he died.

COSTUMES

The men, including Jack Lewis, wear dark suits and ties; the women wear dark, sober dresses.
Catherine Pavic wears a long black shawl.
Emily Black and Robert Holman wear dark sunglasses.

The cavernous interior of a military aircraft hangar.

Mid afternoon.

We see the hangar's interior at a diagonal: on the left, at an acute angle, we can see part of the huge open doorway of the hangar. Outside, the grey tarmac shimmers beneath a sky of brilliant blue.

The back of the stage is dominated by the high, steel wall of the hangar; in the centre of this wall is a set of double doors; there is a window in the top half of each door.

A number of wooden packing cases of various sizes and several oil drums are lined up against the wall.

The rest of the stage is empty.

Sunlight slants in from the hangar's door, creating a large, bright patch of light on the floor.

Silence.

After a pause, BILL*'s face appears at one of the doors, peering into the hangar. He enters. As he quietly closes the door behind him, he checks to see that no-one has followed him. He looks around the hangar, making his way to a low packing crate on which he sits. He puts his hands on his knees and sits staring at them. He sits perfectly still. After a long pause, he hunches his shoulders and slowly bends forward. He makes no sound at first, but gradually a sound begins to escape him: he is wracked with uncontrollable sobs. He covers his face with his hands.*

JACK *appears at the hangar doorway. He carries a toy aeroplane. Seeing* BILL*, he pauses, then takes a few cautious steps towards him.* BILL *is unaware of* JACK*'s presence.* JACK *stops, still some way from* BILL*. He stands watching him for a long moment, then suddenly turns and quickly leaves the hangar.*

BILL*'s sobbing begins to subside. He takes a deep breath, takes a handkerchief from his pocket and wipes his face. He stands up, straightens his clothes, runs his hand through his hair, puts the handkerchief back in his pocket. He walks back towards the double doors, looks out through* *the window, takes another deep breath and leaves, closing the door quietly behind him.*

Silence.

After a pause, TOM *enters through the hangar doorway, mopping his forehead with a white handkerchief.* JACK *holds* TOM*'s other hand. Jack's toy aeroplane is tucked under his arm. As they enter* JACK *looks around the hangar, searching for* BILL.

TOM: I just need to get out of the sun for a while, Jack. And away from all those bloody uniforms. I've never seen so many medals. They'd weigh a man down, wouldn't they? Pretty, though, very pretty, the coloured ribbons and everything shining. We'll sit down here for a minute.

> *They sit on one of the crates.*

You don't want to be a soldier, do you, Jack?

> JACK *shrugs.*

I know your mum… your mum doesn't want you to be. Your dad wasn't sure. He liked the life, but he wasn't sure it was the kind of thing for you. But you'll make up your own mind, one day.

> *Pause.*

You haven't said much today.

> JACK *shakes his head.*

That's alright, if you don't feel like talking you don't have to.

JACK: Nope.

> *Pause.*

TOM: When your dad was your age he was a real blabbermouth. You couldn't shut him up. Yak, yak, yak. Half the time I didn't know what he was talking about. He talked about everything under the sun. He was a great collector of facts. He remembered things. Usually they were completely unimportant things. He knew the average length of a magpie's beak and the weight of a twenty-cent piece. But do you think he could remember his seven times tables?

JACK *shakes his head.*

Of course he couldn't.

Pause.

You'll have to be brave today, Jack.

JACK *nods.*

We'll all have to be as brave as we can. Like your father was.

Pause.

He was a good son. He told me that you were too. He was very proud of you, like I was of him.

He draws JACK *close to his side.*

JACK *buries his face in* TOM*'s shoulder;* TOM *wraps his arms around him.*

Fade to darkness.

In the darkness:

EVE: I'm not quite ready yet… to be with all those people.

HELEN: That's okay.

EVE: I've been dreading today, I really have.

HELEN: I've tried not to think about it.

Lights rise on EVE *and* HELEN.

EVE: Yes, you can think about things too much sometimes.

Pause.

Do you think… I mean… will I be allowed to see Peter's body?

HELEN: I don't know, Eve.

EVE: I mean, I'm his sister and I can ask… to see him, can't I?

Pause.

HELEN: I don't know what there is to see.

Long pause.

EVE: All the funeral arrangements are made.

HELEN: I know.

EVE: My mother is staying with her sister. Her sister won't be coming. She doesn't go to funerals. She's been to too many she says. All her friends are gone. She's getting on of course. I forget how old she is. Seventy something. She says that the next funeral she goes to will be her own. She's a funny old stick. Tough as old boots of course. They all are, all that side of the family.

HELEN: I know.

EVE: Do you want to see his body?

HELEN: No. I don't.

EVE: You might be right. That might be best. I mean, I'd like to remember him... the way he was... you know... the way he was. He was so handsome, wasn't he? Of course you thought he was, I know you did. You always did. I remember the first time you two went out together. Where did you go? I can't remember where you went. You were wearing a blue dress, with a... a scarf, what colour was your scarf? He was so handsome.

She covers her face with her hands.

HELEN *comes close to her and puts her arm around* EVE*'s shoulder.*

HELEN: Yes, he was.

EVE *takes her hands from her face and composes herself.*

EVE: Are you okay, Helen, are you alright?

HELEN: No.

EVE: Of course not. No. Neither am I.

HELEN *takes* EVE*'s hand in hers.*

Fade to darkness.

Lights rise on ROBERT *and* MARTIN.

MARTIN: What does it actually mean... to honour the dead?

ROBERT: It means you don't have to honour the living.

He shrugs.

I don't fucking know, Martin, I really don't. I'm still trying to... come to terms with everything.

Pause.

MARTIN: I still can't believe David's gone, Uncle Rob. Maybe the ceremony today... will make it seem more real.

ROBERT: It's real, mate.

Pause.

Your mum and dad were the first ones I told. I wanted to tell you as well, but your mum thought it would be best coming from her. She was probably right.

Pause.

MARTIN: Dad was pretty cut up.

ROBERT: He takes bad news very hard. Even when we were kids, he was like that. I was always a bit more... stoic.

MARTIN: You don't... I mean, after seeing how dad was so cut up about David... you don't seem to—

ROBERT: You know how I can't be you...?

MARTIN: What?

ROBERT: You know how I can't be you? You can't be me either.

Pause.

MARTIN: You can't be me and I can't be you.

ROBERT: That's right, Martin.

MARTIN: What do you mean?

ROBERT: Just think about it.

MARTIN: Is it a game of some kind?

ROBERT: What? No.

MARTIN: It sounds like a riddle.

ROBERT: It's not a bloody riddle. It's the truth. For fuck's sake...

MARTIN: You don't have to get angry.

ROBERT: There are people, there are lots of people, who want to drill holes in your fucking head. So they can look inside and see what you're thinking.

MARTIN: Why do they want to do that?

ROBERT: To see if you're human. But it's only their idea of what a human is. What they fail to understand is that no two people are the same. You can't be me. Do you see what I'm saying?

MARTIN: Sure, I guess so.

ROBERT: I was there when David was born. I held him in my hands. Look at these hands, they're the same hands... and there are people telling me what I should feel. How can they tell me that?

MARTIN: What people?

ROBERT: I get looks, Martin. I get... hateful looks. They drill holes in my head. Am I going to weep? Who should I weep for? Your father can weep. I can't.

MARTIN: It's okay, Uncle Rob....

ROBERT: I held David in my hands but I can't weep for him. When he was small he was dearer to me than my life... but when he was a grown man he was like a stranger.

MARTIN: He was just... David.

> *Pause.*

ROBERT: A man's worth nothing if he can't keep close what he loves.

> *Blackout.*

> *Lights rise on* BILL *and* TOM LEWIS.

BILL: How've you been, Tom?

TOM: Not too good, Bill, to tell the truth.

> *Pause.*

BILL: Have the boys been with you?

TOM: They've stayed pretty close. Jim's the one who's...

> *Pause.*

Steve and him were as thick as thieves you know.

> *Pause.*

BILL: You've been lucky with your boys. They've always been close. Brothers aren't always that way.

> *Pause.*

TOM: How've you been?

BILL: I've been keeping pretty much to myself since I heard about Steven. I haven't felt like talking to anyone. The people I know... the friends I have... they don't know... I mean, he's nothing to them.

I don't talk about my family very often. I've got no real connections
there. But it's warmer up north.

TOM: It was good of you to come today. I appreciate it.

BILL: I wanted to be here for you and the boys.

Pause.

TOM: Did you come by train?

BILL: Yes, I caught the train.

TOM: It's no more expensive to fly these days.

BILL: I like the train. It gives you time to think.

TOM: How much did it put you out?

TOM *reaches inside his jacket.*

BILL: I won't take your money.

TOM: The pension's not much.

BILL: I appreciate it, but I'm alright.

Pause.

TOM: It's been a while.

BILL: Yes, it has.

TOM: We were close... as young blokes.

BILL: Yes, we were.

Pause.

I don't know what to say.

TOM: There's nothing to say. Steve's gone. That's all there is to it.

Pause.

BILL: If you feel like talking...

TOM: I've talked to the boys. I've tried to help them get through all this.
I haven't got much else to say.

BILL: Who's helping you?

TOM: No-one can help me, Bill. I'm broken into little fucking pieces.

Fade to darkness.

Lights rise on SAM LEWIS *and* JOHN BLACK.

JOHN: G'day.

SAM: Hi.

JOHN *offers his hand.*

JOHN: John. John Black.

SAM: Sam Lewis.

They shake hands.

Pause.

JOHN: Who are you here for?

SAM: My brother, Steve.

JOHN: I'm here for my brother too. Alan.

Pause.

Fucking sad day, isn't it?

SAM: Yeah, it is.

Pause.

JOHN: So you're… younger than your brother?

SAM: Yeah.

JOHN: I'm older than mine. Quite a few years older.

Pause.

It's funny, all of that.

SAM: What?

JOHN: Our brothers won't get any older. So I'll always be older than my brother, but it's not the same for you, I mean you're younger than your brother now, but you'll be older than him, eventually, so instead of you being the younger brother, which you are now, you'll end up being the older brother, like I am. But I can never be the younger brother.

SAM: I guess not.

JOHN: Sorry. I don't know what I'm talking about. I've been talking for days. I don't know what I've been saying, I just keep talking.

SAM: It's okay.

Pause.

JOHN: It's bullshit, all of this. All these flags and brass bands.

SAM: It's just a kind of recognition.

JOHN: Of what?

SAM: Of their lives, I guess. Of the… sacrifice our brothers made. That's important, isn't it?

JOHN: To who?

SAM: Maybe just to them.

JOHN: They were wasted, mate. They were fucking wasted. They had to scrape my brother off the road with a fucking shovel. What was left of him…

Pause.

SAM: I'm angry too.

JOHN: Fuck that. It's no good being angry.

Pause.

My old man fought in the Second World War. He had medals and everything. He survived, he came home. He was a fucking arsehole. But my brother's not coming home.

SAM: I'm sorry.

JOHN: It's no good being sorry.

Pause.

It's just a sad day. That's all.

Pause.

SAM: Is your father here?

JOHN: Him? He doesn't know what day it is. I tried to tell him about Alan. He doesn't remember Alan. He only remembers me now and then, the poor old shit. He'll be gone soon. I think he wants to go. But he keeps hanging on. He can't help himself. He's a survivor. It breaks my fucking heart every time I see him.

Pause.

Smoke?

SAM: Pardon?

JOHN: Do you smoke?

SAM: No.

JOHN: I'm going outside for a smoke. What time's this plane supposed to arrive?

SAM: I was told that there was a delay of some kind in Baghdad. I'm not sure how long it—

JOHN: As long as it turns up.

SAM: I'm sure it'll turn up.

JOHN: See you later, then.

SAM: Yeah, okay, see you later.

> JOHN *goes*.
>
> SAM *remains alone*.
>
> *Blackout*.
>
> *In the darkness*:

I stay among things that have gone;
what has ceased does not cease for me.

> *Lights rise on* SAM, *alone*.

My brother is swallowed in his death,
his baffled cry still echoing,
footprints still hardening in his blood.
The days at least are merciful;
I lose only what's already lost.
But at night the darkness blazes
with the music of his voice;
our games have never ended,
the rubber ball we bounced
pounds inside my chest,
our game of hide and seek
ends only when I wake
still searching for his hiding place.

> *Blackout*.
>
> *Lights rise on* CATHERINE *and* EMILY.

CATHERINE: Were you married long?

EMILY: Two years.

CATHERINE: Was it difficult… deciding to marry a soldier?

EMILY: I didn't think about it. He was a soldier when I met him. He was
    just... himself.
CATHERINE: I didn't want Rik to join the army.
EMILY: Is that your son?
CATHERINE: Yes.

Pause.

I couldn't talk him out of it, no matter how much I tried. I suppose
I should have been pleased that I'd raised a son who knew his own
mind, but that's not what I felt.

Pause.

I understood that he was free of me, finally. The most difficult thing to
accept was that I was also free of him... and that I didn't particularly
want to be.

Pause.

EMILY: I'm sorry... but I noticed that you're alone and I wondered did
    your son... did Rik know his father?
CATHERINE: Don't be sorry. No, he didn't know his father. I hardly
    knew him.
EMILY: Does his father know... what's happened?
CATHERINE: I don't imagine he does.
EMILY: Will you tell him?
CATHERINE: I don't know where he is. Rik was never interested in
    knowing who his father was. He might have been, later, perhaps.
    When he was ready to know.

Pause.

What will you tell her about her father?
EMILY: How do you know it's a girl?
CATHERINE: Something in your face.
EMILY: What?
CATHERINE: I mustn't say.

Pause.

EMILY: I'll tell her that I loved him.

Pause.

CATHERINE: Be your daughter's mother. Do that as well as you can.

Pause.

EMILY: I miss him.

CATHERINE: So will she. That will be enough.

Blackout.

In the darkness:

ALICE: Have you been drinking?

JOHN: I had a couple before I left home.

ALICE: What time was that?

Lights rise on ALICE *and* JOHN.

JOHN: What's it matter what time it was?

ALICE: Did you have to drink?

JOHN: Am I… impaired? I'm standing up, aren't I? My hands are steady, my vision's good. I haven't punched anyone in the fucking mouth.

ALICE: You usually do that on Friday nights.

JOHN: What's it got to do with you anyway?

ALICE: I expected you to turn up sober at least. Couldn't you even do that?

JOHN: I'm here, aren't I?

ALICE: Gutless.

JOHN: What?

ALICE: You're gutless.

Pause.

JOHN *walks away.*

He stops and lights a cigarette, his back to ALICE.

You can't smoke in here.

He turns to face her.

JOHN: You know what I like about you, sis? I like how you're always right. I wish I could always be right. But you know why you're always right? Because you're so afraid of being wrong. It scares the shit out of you. It doesn't scare me at all, because I'm used to it.

ALICE: You're talking through your arse.

JOHN: You haven't said a word about Alan.

Pause.

Not a word.

ALICE: What is there to say?

JOHN: There's got to be something to say.

ALICE: Why?

JOHN: He's our brother.

Pause.

ALICE: You make me laugh, John, you really do.

JOHN: I'm glad I amuse you.

ALICE: What was the last thing you said to Alan?

JOHN: Goodbye?

ALICE: You called him a fool.

JOHN: He was a fool.

ALICE: He was afraid, John. Why do you think he came to you? He was being sent to the Middle East.

JOHN: He was a soldier, wasn't he?

ALICE: And soldiers can't be afraid? He came to you…

JOHN: What for? What could I do for him?

ALICE: You could have been strong for him. But you were more frightened than he was. You were fucking weak and you cursed him.

JOHN: I didn't fucking—

ALICE: You were so afraid of losing him that you turned your back on him.

JOHN: I didn't turn my back.

ALICE: You told him that he was a fool with no mind of his own, that he didn't have the guts to say no.

JOHN: Listen, Alice, you don't—

ALICE: He didn't want to say no, John. He said yes. He wanted to go. I don't know why and it's too late to care. He knew you didn't agree with him, but he wanted your blessing. But you weren't strong enough to give him that. And now you can't even show up to bring his body home without filling yourself with booze and bullshit. You want me to say something about Alan? Why? What I feel is my fucking business. I'm not going to help you, John. Just like you didn't help him.

JOHN: Alice…

> ALICE *approaches* JOHN.

ALICE: Take that cigarette out of you mouth, you prick.

> *He takes the cigarette from his mouth.*

> *She slaps him across the face.*

I loved my brother.

> *Pause.*

JOHN: And what about me?

> *Pause.*

ALICE: You loved him too.

JOHN: That's what I can't… that's what I can't…

> *She embraces him.*

> *Blackout.*

> *Lights rise on* CATHERINE *and* BILL.

BILL: I think that's what… I think that's the worst thing of all. If you know a boy, a little boy, and then you know… the man he becomes… you don't forget the boy. In the death of the man is the death of the child.

> *Pause.*

In the place where our boys died, children die every day. But of course, they're not our children, are they?

> *Pause.*

If you've seen children together, you see how they can be cruel to each other, you see how they can be kind. Their world isn't small just because they are. It's vast and very frightening and very beautiful, and I just think that if we could only recall what it was like…

Pause.

I've never had any children of my own. But I can imagine what it's like. I wish that I couldn't.

Pause.

I'm not making any sense, I know. I don't feel like making sense. I don't feel like saying what I'm supposed to say.

CATHERINE: What are you supposed to say?

BILL: The right things, the proper things, whatever they are. What are we supposed to feel? Our children are dead. I can't endure it. I refuse to.

Pause.

CATHERINE: I don't even know your name.

BILL: I don't know yours.

She offers her hand; BILL *takes it.*

CATHERINE: Catherine.

BILL: Mine's Bill.

CATHERINE: I'm pleased to meet you, Bill.

BILL: After today, we'll probably never see each other again.

CATHERINE: No.

They let go of each other's hand.

Fade to darkness:

Lights rise on EVE *and* HELEN.

EVE: You know what I can't stop thinking about? I wonder… did he kill anyone? He might have had to. He never talked about things like that. I never asked him about it. But that was part of his job, wasn't it? That was always something that might happen. He might have to kill someone. I can't imagine what that would be like. I don't suppose he could imagine it either. Until he had to actually do it. He wasn't up in the air in a plane or anything, those men don't see who they kill, he was right there on the ground with a gun in his hand and anything could happen to him at any moment and he'd have to be ready to kill someone. But did he? I wish I could stop thinking about it. I don't know why I think about it all the time. I want to think about him, I want to think about Peter, I want to think about my brother, the brother that I knew who didn't kill anyone and who never thought about killing anyone and who wouldn't, he wouldn't ever…

Pause.

HELEN: What if you knew that he did?

EVE: But I—

HELEN: What if you did know?

EVE: I'd feel… I'd feel sorry that he had to.

HELEN: But you wouldn't have the right to feel sorry.

EVE: Of course I would.

HELEN: Some things about Peter aren't anything to do with you, or with me. I loved him, Eve, but if he killed people, I'll never know how he felt about it. And maybe he wouldn't want me to know.

Pause.

Believe whatever comforts you, Eve. It's too late for anything else. It was too late the day they left for the Middle East. Believe whatever comforts you.

EVE: What if nothing does?

Fade to darkness.

Lights rise on BILL *and* JIM.

BILL: Even a weak man can love someone. Even an unhappy man can know what happiness is like. If I'm inadequate, that doesn't mean that I don't understand how I'm inadequate.

JIM: Uncle Bill, you're not—

BILL: No, Jim. Listen to me. I can talk to you. At least, I feel that I can.

JIM: Of course you can.

BILL: The man who fails knows that he's failed.

Pause.

I'm lonely and I have regrets; I can't often say what I feel and I often say things that mean nothing to me.

JIM: Everyone does that.
BILL: Not today. We can't do that today.

   Pause.

I've known beautiful things. They stab at me and accuse me. My life's not beautiful.

   Pause.

As old as I am, perhaps I'm still afraid of life, Jim. Life is like a wound that I tend.

   Pause.

I think that for me... love is only a thing to staunch the wound.

   Pause.

I love my brother, but I don't know how to console him. I can't even seem to lift my arms to... to hold him. I don't know why. I want to say something to him... but I can barely talk to him. I love your father, Jim, but suddenly I feel like I don't know him. Or is it me I don't know? I'm a little lost, really I am. I don't know what to do at all.

   Pause.

JIM: You could give me a hug.
BILL: Dear Jim... dear boy.

   They embrace.

JIM: We'll be okay, won't we?
BILL: We'll find a way through this... this terrible time. People do, don't they?

   They part.

JIM: And on the other side of this terrible time... what will there be?
BILL: I don't know. I know that you and Steven were very close.

   Pause.

JIM: I wanted him to always be there.
BILL: No-one can always be there, my boy.
JIM: Why can't they?

Pause.

You know what I fucking hate?

He jabs his finger at his head.

This. I hate this. I'm so fucking clever. I'd rather be stupid. I'd rather howl like a dog. I want to scream my brother's name until he comes home. But I'm clever. Like a rat. No, no-one can always be there. My brother threw his fucking life away. No he didn't. He abandoned me. No he didn't, Jim, don't be stupid. I want to be stupid. I don't want to know the reasons or the whys or the wherefores. I don't want his death justified or this… this fucking grief explained to me.

BILL: Jim… Jim… please…

JIM: I want my fucking brother, Bill, I want my brother and I don't care if he's dead, do you hear me, I don't care if he's fucking dead.

Blackout.

Lights rise on CATHERINE, *alone.*

CATHERINE: They'll carve his name in stone,
   why not here in my breast?
   Why not here in the palm of my hand?
   I'll wear his absence on my face,
   why not his name?
   There is a flame that burns
   for dead soldiers;
   what feeds the flame of remembrance?
   The living are the fuel that memory burns.
   We burn more slowly than the dead;
   our crematoria are the beds we sleep in,
   the streets we walk,
   the rooms where we wait
   for the son who is not returning.
   We leave a trail of ashes
   that are slowly scattered by the wind.

Fade to darkness.

Lights rise on EMILY *and* HELEN.

HELEN: His hair. The colour of his hair.
EMILY: His hands resting on the table.
HELEN: His shoes under the kitchen chair.
EMILY: His footsteps.
HELEN: The smell of him.
EMILY: The weight of him.

> *Pause.*

HELEN: When you say his name…
EMILY: I say his name.
HELEN: When you say his name… can you hardly say his name? As if it's wrong, or as if when you say it you're asking… you're asking him to answer… but he can't answer.

> *Pause.*

EMILY: I say his name in the dark. I whisper it to myself. I'm not asking for anything.

> *Pause.*

HELEN: I sleep on his side of the bed.
EMILY: Me too.
HELEN: When he was away I did that.
EMILY: Yes, when he was away.
HELEN: Now I sleep there. It's my side now.
EMILY: Yes, where he was. I do too.

> *Pause.*

Alan told me that he whispered my name in the dark.
HELEN: Peter whispered mine as well.

> *Fade to darkness.*

> *In the darkness:*

His body was the shape of my touch,
his mouth the shape of my kiss.

> *Lights rise on* HELEN.

We lived in our own country
and knew each other's seasons.

His body was naked as air,
His hands a harbour and a sea.

Our bed was a wild garden
where my eyes were mirrored in his.

We drank from each other's bodies
and slept in each other's silence.

How should I remember him?
Who should I tell that I loved him?

> *Blackout.*

> *Lights rise on* JOHN, ROBERT *and* TOM.

JOHN: I've tried to tell my father. But I can't get through to him. The poor bugger doesn't even remember his own name.

TOM: It must be a pretty miserable existence.

ROBERT: Maybe it's peaceful, not knowing anything.

JOHN: I doubt he knows who I am anymore. Sometimes I kid myself that he does, but it's like I'm not there, and he's not there either.

TOM: But he is there, that's the thing. So are you.

ROBERT: What can he do if his own father doesn't know who he is?

TOM: I don't suppose that there's anything he can do.

JOHN: There's nothing I can do.

TOM: But you're someone who visits him. You show an interest. That's something.

JOHN: At least he doesn't know Alan's gone.

TOM: He lost Alan, and you, some time ago.

JOHN: And we lost him.

> *Pause.*

> ROBERT *is suddenly isolated in a pool of light.*

ROBERT: I knew… before they told me. I knew. I woke up one morning and I knew that David was dead. It was so… overwhelming. And the funny thing was that I suddenly felt closer to him than I'd been in a long time. Me and David didn't get along that well. I don't know why. There was an ocean between us. It was really like that.

We had nothing to say to each other. But that morning when I woke up I was shaking... and I felt something drain out of me. That's the only way I can describe it. Something drained out of me and it was David's life, all the energy and the anger and the fucking beauty of it. I'd locked it up in here, somewhere here inside of me and then I felt it drain out of me. But I felt it, at least I fucking felt it.

Blackout.

In the darkness:

TOM: What's left of my son?
What's in that box draped in a flag?
Have they managed
to stitch anything together?

Lights rise on TOM, *alone.*

Does it even resemble a body?
Does it matter?
I remember holding his hand.
That was in another life.
But it was my life.
My son in my arms is something I've felt;
my son's voice is something I've heard.
I've seen his shoulders broaden,
his voice darken with manhood.
I want to see my son again.
I don't want to remember him,
I want him in my arms
dead or living,
the bright, grave joy of his youth,
his going away and his coming home again.
I want my son.

Blackout.

Lights rise on JIM, SAM *and* TOM. JACK *is a little way off, sitting on the ground playing with his toy aeroplane.*

JIM: Are you okay, Dad?

TOM: Are you?

JIM: I just want to get all of this over with.

TOM: I know.

SAM: I don't… feel anything. I mean… about any of this.

TOM: It's just a ceremony.

JIM *looks over towards* JACK.

Pause.

JIM: His mum should be here.

SAM: Why?

JIM: If not for Steve, then for Jack at least.

TOM: Jack's got all the family he needs.

JIM: She should be here.

TOM: I talked to her. I didn't try to convince her to come. I listened to what she had to say.

JIM: What did she say?

TOM: She'll be at the funeral tomorrow. You can ask her yourself.

JIM: I don't want to talk to her.

SAM: I don't get it, Jim.

JIM: What?

SAM: Do you want to be here?

Pause.

JIM: No. I don't know. Yes.

SAM: She didn't want to be here, so she's not.

Pause.

JIM: But being here… it's supposed to mean something.

TOM: What?

JIM: I was hoping you could tell me.

Pause.

TOM: Five men are coming home together. They're coming home together because they died together. They were mates, probably. And a fuss has to be made. Does anybody believe that they died defending their country? But they must have died for some reason. That's a bit of a problem really. Because maybe they actually died for no good reason at all. And the best way to hide that fact is to make a fuss about their deaths. No-one will ask why they died if enough fuss is made about the fact that they're dead. That'll be enough.

Pause.

It's a terrible thing to say, but we owe it to the dead to say it for them. They died for no good reason. No-one will hear us say it. But we'll know it. And knowing it will have to be enough.

JIM: Enough for what?

TOM: Maybe it's enough to know the truth, even if you can't say it, even if no-one would listen if you did.

Pause.

Five mates are coming home today. They're coming home to be forgotten. Their names will be written in stone.

Fade to darkness.

Lights rise on ALICE, *alone.*

ALICE: As children we
were thick as thieves,
on the garage roof
spitting and chucking stones.
He laughed at things
I didn't laugh at.
I never saw him cry.
We vowed we'd stay
best friends.

There was a distance finally
broad and empty,
our younger faces
shimmering there.

He was kind to me
when we met, always,

and I loved the way
his face kept changing as he grew
into the fullness of himself,

that broken promise.

Fade to darkness.

Lights rise on ALICE *and* EMILY.

EMILY: Alan didn't want me to know too much about his army life. He didn't want me to imagine where he was or who he was with. He didn't want me to think about him while he was away.

ALICE: What were you supposed to do?

EMILY: Invent another life, with no Alan in it. He said that would be the best thing.

ALICE: That's a terrible thing to ask.

EMILY: Alan always asked a lot of the people he loved, and if you loved him, you did the best you could.

ALICE: What did you ask of him?

EMILY: That he'd come home safe.

Pause.

It's hard not to think about him, or the sound of his voice or the way that he touched me, but I mustn't do that. I'm alone now.

ALICE: Em, you're not alone.

EMILY: I know. I've never been alone and I'll never be alone. And I'm so ungrateful. People are so kind. I should stop thinking about him. I should stop wondering who was the last person he spoke to, the last person to touch him, or who was the last person to look into his eyes.

ALICE: You were.

Pause.

EMILY: How could I be?

ALICE: You were the last person to look into his eyes.

Pause.

EMILY: Was I?

ALICE: Yes, you were.

Fade to darkness.

In the darkness:

JOHN: If you need anything, just let me know.

EMILY: I will.

Lights rise on JOHN *and* EMILY.

JOHN: Just let me know. I'll be around, Em. I'll stay close.

EMILY: You don't have to.

JOHN: I want to.

Pause.

EMILY: But I don't want you to.

Pause.

JOHN: Why?

EMILY: I want some time alone.

JOHN: But Emily—

EMILY: You asked me if I needed anything. That's what I need.

JOHN: You need your family around you.

EMILY: When was the last time I saw you?

JOHN: I've been slack, I know.

EMILY: I don't expect anything from you, John. Neither did Alan.

JOHN: Emily…

EMILY: Why don't we just leave it at that?

JOHN: I can't.

Pause.

I want to be with my family. Alice has been giving me all this shit… maybe I deserve it. But why should I only have what I deserve?

Pause.

I let Alan down. I want to make up for it.

EMILY: You can't.

Pause.

I'm sorry, John.

JOHN: Yeah. We're all sorry. What's done's done.

EMILY: No. Some things are never finished.

Fade to darkness.

Lights rise on JACK, *alone.*

He holds his toy aeroplane high over his head and runs around the hangar; he dives and swoops the plane; he brings it in to land on one of the crates, then takes off again.

CATHERINE *appears in the hangar doorway. She watches* JACK, *who is at first unaware of her. When he sees her he stops playing and stands still, tucking the plane under his arm.*

CATHERINE *walks towards him. She leans close to him and speaks softly.* JACK *nods.*

CATHERINE *sits on one of the crates and watches* JACK *as he resumes his game, swooping and diving his plane as he runs around the hangar.*

Fade to darkness.

Lights rise on ROBERT, *alone.*

ROBERT: I hear the voice of my son calling.
    He looks homewards to me
    where I burn
    in the suspended nightmare of his loss,
    not yet able to scream, nor weep nor curse.
    My son calls me
    and I answer him:
    come home to me now,
    bring your lost life
    to grief's foundry,
    we'll forge a meaning from it;
    the hammer of my tears
    on the anvil of your blood.
    It is the labour that matters,
    the shaping out of emptiness
    the necessary presence of your death.

Blackout.

Lights rise on JACK, *alone, asleep on one of the crates.*

JIM *and* SAM *appear in the hangar doorway.*

SAM: I saw him come in here.

JIM: I told the little bugger to stay with us.

SAM: He's bored.

JIM: We're supposed to stay in the official...

SAM: Enclosure.

JIM: We're supposed to stay there.

SAM: The plane's an hour late, at least. Nobody cares where we go. They'll call us when... they need us.

    They see JACK.

There he is. He's out to it.

    They approach JACK.

JIM: Poor little shit.

    JIM *sits beside* JACK; *he strokes* JACK's *hair.*

SAM: He should have stayed at home.

    Pause.

Maybe we all should have.

JIM: Why?

SAM: This is all just...

    He shrugs.

It's just a show. Isn't it?

JIM: I'm here for Steve.

SAM: He's not going to know you are.

JIM: But I know I am.

SAM: Do you think that makes any difference, I mean to anyone but you?

JIM: Dad needs me.

SAM: What can you do for Dad?

    Pause.

JIM: Nothing.

Pause.

SAM: Why should we be here, Jim? To keep up appearances?
JIM: It's our brother they're bringing home.
SAM: But he's not actually coming home, is he?

> SAM *turns and starts to leave.*

> JIM *stands.*

JIM: Then why are you here? Sam?

> SAM *stops and turns to him.*

Why are you here?
SAM: I'm here because you are, Jim.
JIM: But why are you fucking here?

> *Pause.*

SAM: Because you're my brother and I love you.

> *He turns and leaves.*

> JIM *sits beside* JACK *again; he strokes* JACK*'s hair.*

> *He weeps.*

> *Fade to darkness.*

> *In the darkness:*

JIM: Where are my brother's eyes
　　that saw me just born,
　　his hands trusted to hold me?

> *Lights slowly rise, revealing* JIM *holding* JACK, *asleep, in his arms.*

Before I opened my eyes
lying in his arms I knew him,
I felt his heart beat.

I dream that my brother
falls endlessly towards me,
a hawk shearing the high air.

Where are his eyes, his hands?
Lightly, as if it might break
he held my hand as I stumbled
out of babyhood to walk beside him.
Where is my brother's voice
that called me home from play,
that cajoled me and bickered
and told me secrets?

He falls towards me
through the high air.

> *Blackout.*

> *In the darkness, the sound of an approaching aeroplane is heard;
> a dull roar, slowly increasing in volume.*

> *Lights rise on* CATHERINE, *alone.*

CATHERINE: We are strangers
in a new and darker world.

> JACK *appears in the hangar doorway, still holding his toy aero-
> plane;* CATHERINE *turns to him.*

Is it time to go?
JACK: Yep.

> JACK *approaches.* CATHERINE *holds out her hand;* JACK *takes it.*

CATHERINE: Now we'll learn our grief, waiting
for those not coming home
to come home none the less.
We'll make new lives
and learn to live with emptiness.

> *They turn and walk towards the hangar door.* JACK *lifts the toy
> aeroplane above his head, flying it through the air.*

> *The noise of the approaching aeroplane increases to a deafening
> roar.*

The light outside grows to a blinding intensity as JACK *and* CATHERINE *leave the hangar. They dissolve in a blaze of light.*

Outside, a brass band begins to play the national anthem.

Blackout and silence.

THE END